The Loneliest Place in the Universe

Brian Fence

To my mother and father,
may they both rest in peace.

These poems deal with heartache, depression, and themes like alcoholism. I was inspired by a lost love and the alcohol abuse of my mother. While some may be a bit gritty, these poems come from the heart and represent my transition into new happiness with my husband. Some were painful to write, but I found it cathartic to share my work with my peers and anyone else who enjoys poetry and some melancholy.

Table of Contents

Table of Contents	*4*
"The Ballad of Miss Monique"	*5*
"Dear John"	*6*
"My Little Johnny"	*8*
"Pasta alla Giovanni — Some Whimsy at Love Lost"	*9*
"Open"	*10*
"Runaway"	*11*
"Our Night's Pantoum"	*12*
"The Loneliest Place in the Universe"	*14*
"Corners"	*15*
"Tanka 1"	*16*
"Tanka 2"	*17*
"Tanka 3"	*18*
"Gin and Tanka"	*19*
"Mama's Lover"	*20*
"Beard"	*21*
"Pixelation"	*22*
"Abroad"	*23*
"Gochisou"	*24*
"Hiroshima"	*25*
"third culture kid"	*26*

"The Ballad of Miss Monique"

On Friday nights she takes the stage,
The lovely Miss Monique.
Knock-out curves and diamond eyes
Seduce you with mystique.

For many a year from dusk till dawn
She owned the circuit scene.
A Cosmopolitan top or bottom,
And everything in between.

When Miss Monique is on parade
Groins gyrate to her song;
The men invite her yielding lips
But she never loves them long.

Sorry, boys, you'll have to wait —
I've no time left to play.
Tonight I need my beauty sleep;
Tomorrow's another day!

But a thousand mornings later
Makeup could no longer hide
The hollowed eyes and misery
Of the nameless man inside.

So all the men who had loved her so
Abandoned sweet Monique.
Once runner-up Miss Gay PA,
Forgotten within a week.

"Dear John"

We tucked two hearts in hole and in corner,
And shared our secrets in shades of pale blue.
I started balancing life on your chest
That night we set on a quest to spy the moon,
Equipped to bless the night so wide with tears
(Or ride your thighs to the brink of the world).

Escape is good for the waifs of the world;
Searched six months straight (not quite) for a corner
Just right to shade me from glint of the tears
You shed as you fled, both unsexed and blue.
Alone I slicked my stomach beneath the moon
Dreaming rather of painting your chest.

But damn my longing for that now-nothing chest,
Its empty barrel splayed wide to the world.
Time to decide I can no longer moon
Over left or right at the street corner
Near you, taking inventory of blue
Irises I gladly watered with tears.

Flowers your husband planted beg me to tear
Their flesh like I tore nails across your chest.
Something old (you), new (me), borrowed (time), blue
Me — me, who pitfalled into Eros' world.
Or rather, I pratfell into a corner
Of a peevishly open honeymoon.

When's it okay to stop loving him, Moon?
When will your tugging stop milking out tears?
I board once more to take a new corner
Stuck with the baggage he checked in my chest
And an invalid passport to his world,
Stamped cover to cover in black and blue.

Last night, I peered up into the deep blue
To be issued a challenge by the moon:
Enshroud your fey-light love below the world
And wash my hands of the oily tears
I used to get you off. My chest
Chose to ignore the throbbing in its corner.

Off in the night's corner I stashed my blue
Vellum suit in a chest, hidden from the moon
And saved my next batch of tears for the world.

"My Little Johnny"

My little pony
My little pony
Fuck me like
Friendship is magic
I used to think you were my very best friend

Like the condoms
(Or restraint) we didn't use
Because your husband said okay
Because Eric — Eros — went away

My little Johnny
My little Johnny
Fuck me like
Love is magic
I used to think you were my very only one.

"Pasta alla Giovanni — Some Whimsy at Love Lost"

You fetid hunk of Parmesan,
I'd aged you for so long:
A year or more my heart's been yours,
Reggiano? Was I wrong.

Rank and stank, umami abound
I lapped up your stupid funk.
The more I loved you and your perfect bite
The more, oh Christ, I sunk.

You'd disappear one day; we knew.
(So would I, for a better bite.) You'd disappear one day; we said:
Just give me that warm plate tonight.

Now when I grate the heady Parmesan
Over my spaghetti *al dente*,
All I'll know is that you've gone,
Grating your heart as you left me.

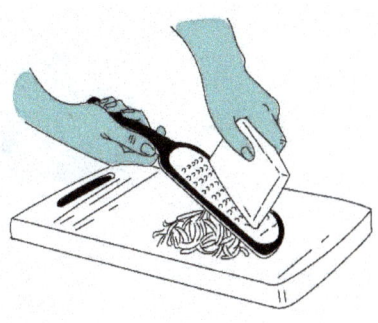

"Open"

My love has gone to jolly Down Under
For pies and chips and Kangaroo footy
And I set out for castles and wonder
To taste of robes and port wine in Blighty.
It's said that nothing tests a good man's heart
Like breaking bad (and beds) on foreign soils;
A ticket to punch before I depart
And sample a stranger's honey-sweet spoils.
While he veered south and I kept to his west
We both unlocked and left a door open;
Every caress of another man's chest
Proved yet another doorframe had broken.
   I dropped my degree in ignorant bliss
   All for the sake of exploring a kiss.

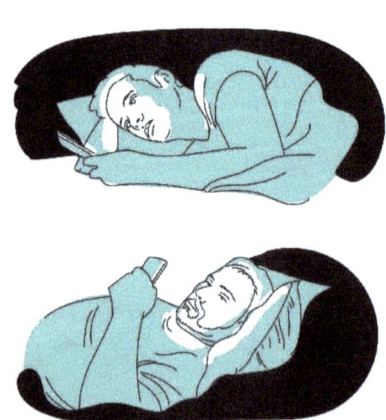

"Runaway"

I wake up slick with sweat
Briny tears, plip-plop-plip, one-by-one
— as it should be —
onto my chest.

My musk smells, tastes like you;
My muscles are stiff from last night.

When we are dead, I say.
An empty room ignores bulging pajamas;
— carnal desire —
to feel you inside me again.

My mind straddles you,
My line between dream and nightmare.

When we are dead, I say.
A visceral longing won't come, it won't
— I yank an unsuspecting pillow —
to prevent sunbeams' queries.

Who did you wake up with,
Who did you wake up with, this morning?

When we are dead, I say,
When we are dead, and then
— I finally realized —
I'd sleep just to run away with you again.

"Our Night's Pantoum"

When you begged me to borrow down the moon,
I pocketed it away for safekeeping.
I would make the night ours forever
So I challenged the sun in the West.

I pocketed it away for safekeeping
(Though it threatened to burn my trousers) —
So I challenged the sun in the West
And I flung its fire into the sea!

Though it threatened to burn my trousers,
My nighttime longing for you lapped me
And I flung its fire into the sea
Carried by a pale wind bound for the North.

My nighttime longing for you lapped me,
Like it was an unctuous ocean.
Carried by a pale wind bound for the North
I veered off-course and found myself South.

Like it was an unctuous ocean,
I paddled the blue-dark sky to the stars.
I veered off-course and found myself South-
Compelled to gather its foxtrot twinkles.

I paddled the blue-dark sky to the stars
Because I wanted to slay the night,
Compelled to gather its foxtrot twinkles
That might have graced your fickle glasz eyes.

Because I wanted to slay the night,
The last place to visit was the East:
That *might* have graced your fickle glasz eyes
—If you had chosen to sail beside me.

The last place to visit was the East
When you begged me to borrow down the
moon. If you had chosen to sail beside me,
I would make the night ours forever.

"The Loneliest Place in the Universe"

The loneliest place in the universe
Lies dimpled between your perfect smile
Your quiet countenance; my jet black hearse
Leaves my cock atwitter all the while.

The loneliest place far behind the moon
Where hearts beat at 2.7 Kelvin
Confirms my parents' thoughts I'm a buffoon,
To split my heart like a tree most elven.

The loneliest place that is all of God?
Is the joyous void between your damn teeth
Where once my tongue used to welcomely prod
Now is woefully left behind to seethe,

The loneliest place in the universe
Is the space without you: my joy, my curse.

"Corners"

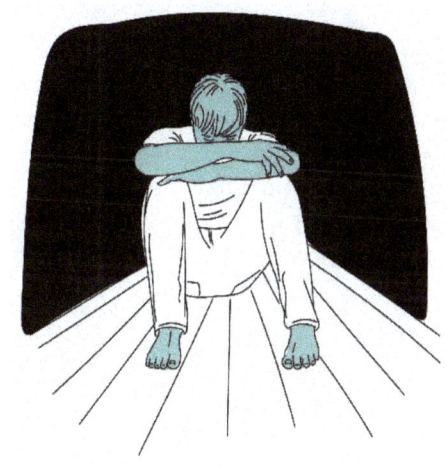

The vice of loss when moon sinks below sea
When your love leaves for the last time
Takes a soul beyond its normal borders
For refuge in lands beyond
We break bread with foreign souls
Hoping that aboard…?
Yearning, hoping to fill the gaping holes
Bore into us by love's selfish departure
North and south; east and west —
To the four corners of the earth
…Escape the steady rhythm of your chest
But beneath every sky I find the loss all the same
The loneliest corner that man has found
Is the corner where love resides now.

"Tanka 1"

bite down; harder!
so I asked for your safety word.
don't need one with you.
my smile was tinctured with rue
knowing we'd need one come morning.

"Tanka 2"

a taunt, a kiss:
words *you little dummy*
show me love
with lips that sweeten
like apple mixed with curry.

"Tanka 3"

an old stain
lingers on a shirt you gave me
your smile appears
reminding me of a time
we could laugh at our mistakes

"Gin and Tanka"

when you think you love
only a neat martini —
then you've drank us all
briny glass, meant to outlast
those who deserve more merit

such juniper eyes
those aren't yours —
are they, mom?
I can smell the sin
and it isn't mine to bare
and it isn't mine to care

the brothers call me
come to hospital for mom
not my shot to take!
give us martini instead —
and leave us both left for dead

"Mama's Lover"

Mama's longtime lover is named Tanqueray;
He's her regular beau and quite debonair.
At night he's with her; I must wait for the day.

Flaccid and forgotten, Papa had to give way:
His monochrome nature could hardly compare
To Mama's longtime lover, named Tanqueray.

My brothers and I have all been betrayed
For a juniper man with dry-tasting hair.
At night he's with her; we must wait for the day.

When the working day ends and sky fades to grey
Mama sets out her glass and begins to prepare
For her longtime lover, named Tanqueray.

It's always at moonrise that he comes to stay,
Leaving bittersweet seed to impregnate the air.
At night he's with her; I must wait for the day.

And he follows me now, invites me to play —
Though I often decline, I am always aware
Of Mama's longtime lover, named Tanqueray.
At night he's with her; I must wait for the day.

"Beard"

Hiding your face with bristles:
Is it the mottles you obscure
Or the quiet tick of your hand
Too unsteady to hold a razor,
Too shaky to pen a sentence.

When self-control fades into a
Niggling voice in your ears
And you wash it away with waters
From the blushful Hippocrene
Staining your pale lips carmine.

If only to scribe a word
In unfettered script
Or drag that razor across
Your face without bleeding drink;
To speak and not slur.

Would you exorcise all your comfort
To gather up the shards of the lost?
Would you sleep alone once
more?
Would you discard him forever:
Your sweet lover named
Tanqueray?

"Pixelation"

The weight of winter, murky oppression:
Woe-stricken air that chirps with strangers' texts
Offering succor from where my thoughts run,
Disturbed unknowns seek pics; I am unsexed.

GPS guides my feet to your front door:
Wine-fueled, unclean fist finds the strength to knock.
Preamble ignored, clothes discarded to floor,
I cry as I come, your hand on my cock.

Finish is messy; guilt bids me to go,
Though craving warm touch, I won't spend the night;
Embracing not your body, but my MacBook Pro,
Awash in shades of purple pixels bright.

An act so childish, I watch my ponies:
An act so simple what saves the lonely.

"Abroad"

the car lurches
we collide in
xenophobic cacophony

nonchalant eyes scan me
I'm just an ad
in the morning paper

foreign boy rides train:
blue jeans and blondeness
on display till 9 am

my lids fold differently
but I am not blind
to life

I stay outside
because it's the only place
not whitewashed

"Gochisou"

love like a full-course dinner

    when late for train
    sticky-sweet onigiri is
    compassion for breakfast

    biting cold
    you say 'okaeri'
    with cherry blossom tea

    drunken daze
    smile-cured hangover
    and puckered umeboshi

sayonara comes and I can't pay the bill

"Hiroshima"

clocks are stopped just before sunrise
locking, locking; locked out of life
is a town of memories
here dead get high off mushroom clouds
donated by the FDA
they never weep for the loss but

in the grey city of ashes
zombied architects are waiting
to plan the next memorial
forgotten children sing a dirge
for the boys down in Washington
who want to break the world again

"third culture kid"

Put me in the oubliette
& shake lose my skin like Sonia Sanchez
I'm so vanilla I'm burnt like the sun
& my beans are worth 17 bucks at whole foods

Put me in the oubliette
& forget me like Hiroshima
I'm so yellow inside I'm burnt as the sun
& my glasses make me smarter than I am

Put me in the oubliette
& doff me like harry potter
I'm so chavvy outside my skin is burnt by the sun
& my tee shirts make me trashier than Primark

Put me in the oubliette
& take away my glass eyes
I'm so lonely inside I'm burnt beneath the sun
& and my heart just wants to be forgotten

www.ingramcontent.com/pod-product-compliance
Lightning Source LLC
Chambersburg PA
CBHW071458070426
42452CB00040B/1882